はじめに

　暮らしの中で、リサイクルやエコロジーなど環境に関する取り組みが行われるようになり、消費者が手にとる商品やブランド、そして企業のイメージも、人や自然に配慮がなされた安全で安心感のあるものが求められるようになりました。

　こうした流れの中で、優しいイメージや雰囲気を伝える広告の重要性が高まってきています。

　本書は、安心感、あたたかさ、優しさ、爽快さ、素朴さ、快適さ、瑞々しさ、リラックス感など、人の心に優しく響くナチュラルな表現をビジュアルとして成功させたデザインを、業種別に紹介していきます。

　業種によって、伝えたいイメージやアプローチ方法は変わってきます。
　たとえば、食品や飲料業界では、安全性に関心が高く、新鮮さと瑞々しさを喚起するフレッシュな色使いや、大地のあたたかさを感じさせる写真が効果的に使われる傾向が見られます。
　ラグジュアリー感とナチュラル感という一見相反するイメージを求められるコスメティックやファッション業界では、オーガニックや無添加を伝えるエコロジカルな素材使いや淡い空気感のある写真で、新しい美の価値観を提案している作品が印象的です。
　そして、日々の暮らしにまつわるインテリアや家電の業界では、自然のモチーフを生かした、自然と人が共存するような安らぎと快適さを演出するデザインが多く見られます。

　安心できる商品やサービスを求める消費者のニーズは、これからも増えていくことでしょう。本書が、時代の要請に応える参考書籍として、さまざまなクリエイターや広告・広報に携わる方々の一助となれば幸いです。

　最後になりましたが、お忙しい中、本書の制作にあたり、素晴らしい作品をご提供くださいましたクリエイターの皆様、および快くご協力を賜りました各社広報・宣伝部門の方々に、心より御礼申し上げます。

ピエ・ブックス編集部

Foreword

Environmental action that includes recycling and ecological awareness is becoming a part of our everyday lives and there is now a demand for companies and for products and brands used by consumers to be friendly towards humans and the environment in addition to being safe and trustworthy.

Amidst all this, advertising that conveys gentle, "natural" images has assumed an ever greater importance.

With an industry-specific structure, this book introduces examples of design that in a visual format has successfully expressed the concepts of "natural" – security, warmth, gentleness, revitalization, simplicity, comfort, freshness, relaxation – that resound softly in the viewer's heart.

The different industries have taken different approaches to conveying the messages they desires to send.

The concept of safety, for example, is a major concern for the food and beverage industry. We see many examples where color schemes evoking the idea of freshness and photographs conveying the warmth of the earth have been used to great effect.

The cosmetics and fashion industry, which at first glance would seem to favor images of luxury that are the opposite of the image of "natural," has impressively created a new set of values for beauty using ecological materials that convey the idea of organic and "additive-free" as well as light and airy photography.

In the home furnishings and household appliance industry so interconnected with our everyday lives, there are many examples of design that have maximized the value of the natural motif and suggest a world where humans and nature exist together with ease and comfort.

There will be an increasing number of consumers looking for products and services that they can feel confident about. We hope that this book will be a useful guide to creators and people involved in advertising and public relations in terms of responding to the demands of the modern world in which we live.

Finally, we want to take this opportunity to express our sincere appreciation to all the creators who took the time to provide us with such splendid examples of their work and the staff in the public relations and advertising departments of various companies for their cooperation in the production of this book.

PIE Books, Editorial Department

editorial note

A カテゴリー Category
B クライアント Client
C 業種 Type of Industry
D スタッフクレジット Staff Credit
   AD: アート・ディレクター Art Director
   CA: クリエイティブ・エージェンシー Creative Agency
   CD: クリエイティブ・ディレクター Creative Director
   CW: コピーライター Copywriter
   D: デザイナー Designer
   DF: デザイン会社 Design Firm
   E-: エグゼクティブ Executive
   I: イラストレーター Illustrator
   P: フォトグラファー Photographer
   PL: 企画者 Planner
   PM: プロダクション・マネージャー Production Manager
   PR: プロデューサー（営業） Producer
   SB: 作品提供社（者） Submittor

※上記以外の制作者呼称は省略せずに掲載しています。
All other production titles are unabbreviated.

※本書に掲載されている店名、店舗写真、販促ツール、商品などは、すべて２００８年１０月時点での情報になります。
All in store-related information, including shop name, photography, promotional items and products are accurate as of October 2008.

※本書に掲載されているキャンペーン、プロモーションは、既に終了しているものもありますので、ご了承ください。
Please note that some campaigns and promotions are no longer deployed.

※作品提供者の意向によりデータの一部を記載していない場合があります。
Please note that some credit information has been omitted at the request of the submittor.

※各企業に附随する、"株式会社、（株）" および "有限会社、（有）" は表記を省略させて頂きました。
The "kabushiki gaisha (K.K., Inc., Co.,Ltd.)" and "yugen gaisha (Ltd.)" portions of all company name have been omitted.

※本書に記載された企業名・商品名は、掲載各社の商標または登録商標です。
The company and product names that appear in this book are published and/or registered trademarks.

RELAXING GRAPHICS WARM, CALM, EXHILARATING

Copyright © 2008 PIE BOOKS
All rights reserved. No part of this publication may be reproduced in any form or by any means, graphic, electronic or mechanical, including photocopying and recording by an information storage and retrieval system, without permission in writing from the publisher.

PIE BOOKS
2-32-4, Minami-Otsuka, Toshima-ku, Tokyo 170-0005 JAPAN
Tel : +81-3-5395-4811 Fax : +81-3-5395-4812

e-mail :
editor@piebooks.com
sales@piebooks.com
http://www.piebooks.com

ISBN978-4-89444-736-3 C3070
Printed in Japan

ナチュラルスタイル グラフィックス

Relaxing Graphics Warm, Calm, Exhilarating

Contents

editorial note	003
foreword	004 - 005
food	010 - 065
beauty	066 - 115
home	116 - 153
others	154 - 183
logo	184 - 189
index	190 - 191

food

キリン KIRIN
食品製造・販売 [Food manufacture and sales]
CD, CW: 谷山雅計 Masakazu Taniyama
AD: 佐野研二郎 Kenjiro Sano
D: 長嶋りかこ Rikako Nagashima / 武田利一 Kazutoshi Takeda
P: 木寺紀雄 Norio Kidera SB: MR_DESIGN

ポスター Posters

ポスター Posters

018 food

Waitrose
スーパーマーケット経営 [Specialty super market]
CD: David Turner & Bruce Duckworth   D: Sam Lachlan (b) / Christian Eager (c, d) / Jamie MacCathie (a)
I: Darren Whittington (a) / Jaques Fabre (d)   P: Steve Baxter (c)   Artwork: Reuben James (d)
Retouching: Peter Ruane (a,c)   DF, SB: Turner Duckworth: London & San Francisco

food 019

b

c

d

food

food   021

Waitrose
スーパーマーケット経営 [Specialty super market]
CD: David Turner & Bruce Duckworth   D: Sam Lachlan (e, g) / Bruce Duckworth (f) / Sarah Moffat (h)   P: Steve Baxter (e) / Andy Grimshaw (g, h)
Artwork: Reuben James (g, h)   Image manipulation: Peter Ruane (e)   Retouch: Peter Ruane (h)   DF, SB: Turner Duckworth, London & San Francisco

022 food

ポスター Posters

ワインビストロ ベルジェ La cave a vin Berger
レストラン [Restaurant]
AD, D: 相澤徳行 Noriyuki Aizawa　DF, SB: 相澤デザイン室 Aizawa Design

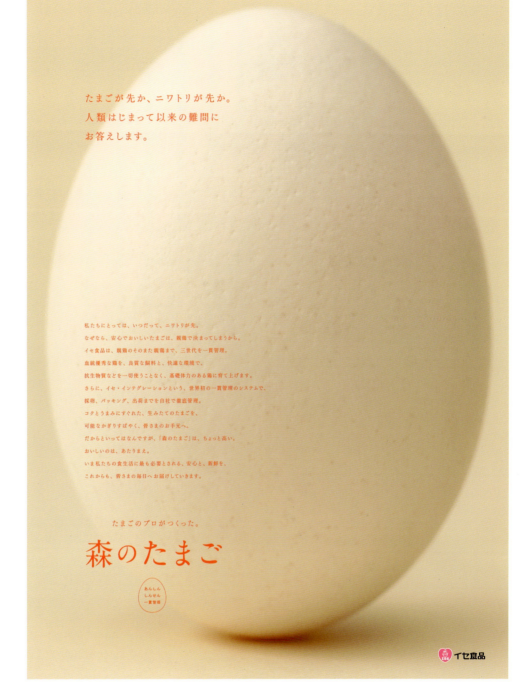

ポスター Posters

イセ食品 ISE FOODS
食料品製造 [Food manufacture]
CD: 本谷一也 Kazuya Mototani　AD: 堀江健一 Kenichi Horie　D: 金原亜伊 Ai Kanehara
P: 伊藤彰浩 Akihiro Ito　CW: 斉藤芳弥 Yoshiya Saito　DF: 青山クリエイティブスタジオ Aoyama Creative Studio
SB: マッキャンエリクソン McCann Erickson Japan

「自然の力を活かしたら、スナックはもっとおいしくできる。」
そう考える私たちには、追求すべきことがまだまだあります。
じゃがいも、にんじん、たまねぎ、かぼちゃ・・・、そして、えび。
自然素材の味わいをそのままに、もっとおいしくできないか。
その生命力を、もっとカラダにとりこめないか。
畑と海の力がつまった新鮮なおいしさを、より早くお届けできないか。
自然の可能性を、スナックフーズの可能性に変えていく。
いま、カルビーの新しい挑戦がはじまっています。

掘りだそう、自然の力。
Calbee

food 025

ポスター Poster

日本マクドナルド McDonald's
ハンバーガー・レストラン・チェーン経営等 [Hamburger chain]
CD: 滝澤てつや Tetsuya Takizawa
AD: 清水克弘 Katsuhiro Shimizu / 中村仁也 Jinya Nakamura / 稲村陽一 Yoichi Inamura
D: 石井謙太朗 Kentaro Ishii / 佐藤健史 Takeshi Sato　P: 白鳥新太郎 Shintaro Shiratori
フード&シズルプランナー: 森沢のり子 Noriko Morisawa
DF: ワタインク WATA INC.　SB: ビーコン・コミュニケーションズ beacon communications

カルビー Calbee Foods
菓子・食品製造・販売 [Food manufacture and sales]
CD: 福島和人 Kazuto Fukushima　AD: 大野耕平 Kohei Ono
D: 中嶋裕治 Yuji Nakajima　P: 児島孝宏 Takahiro Kojima
CW: 加藤大志郎 Taishiro Kato　DF: 博報堂プロダクツ HAKUHODO Product's
SB: カルビー Calbee Foods

026 food

食材を健康にする糖質、トレハロース。

ポスター Posters

H+B ライフサイエンス　H+B LIFE SCIENCE
健康補助食品製造・販売　[Health foods manufacture and sales]
CD: 久米章一　Shoichi Kume　AD: 福島 治　Osamu Fukushima / 矢野智久　Tomohisa Yano
D: 佐々木陽介　Yosuke Sasaki / 村田 渉　Wataru Murata　CW: 河野洋平　Yohei Kouno
SB: 福島デザイン　FUKUSHIMA DESIGN

新聞広告 Newspaper advertisements

カゴメ Kagome
食品製造・販売 [Food manufacture and sales]
CD: 藤木 豊 Yutaka Fujiki AD, D: 齊藤大輔 Daisuke Saito CW: 夏目茂佳 Shigeyoshi Natsume PL: 鈴木みのり Minori Suzuki
P: 佐藤義則 Yoshinori Sato Hair: 河原里美 Satomi Kawahara Make: 島田真理子 Mariko Shimada
PR: 新居康伸 Yasunobu Nii / 佐藤義則 Yoshinori Sato P: 須藤秀之 Hideyuki Suto / 竹浦康郎 Yasuo Takeura
Stylist: 坂元真澄 Masumi Sakamoto / 渡邊美穂 Miho Watanabe
Agency, DF, SB: エージー AZ

Maddy's Organic Meals
産地直送無農薬ベビーフード [Farm fresh organic baby food]
D: Eric Kass   DF, SB: Funnel: Eric Kass: Utilitarian+Commercial+Fine・Art

Firefly Tonics
飲料水製造・販売 [Beverage manufacture and sales]
DF: Firefly in-house team, Burocreative
P: Phillip Spears (Wake up) / Richard Pack (Chill Out) / Terry Vine (Detox) /
John Lund & Sam Diephuis (Health Kick) / Chris Whitehead (Sharpen up)
SB: Firefly Tonics

Chef'n
キッチン用品の製造・販売 [Manufacturer & retailer of specialty kitchen accessories]
CD: Kathy Saito / Jack Anderson / Lisa Cerveny   D. P: Sonja Max
D: Alan Copeland   SB: Hornall Anderson

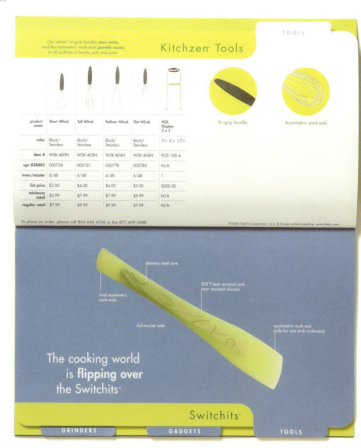
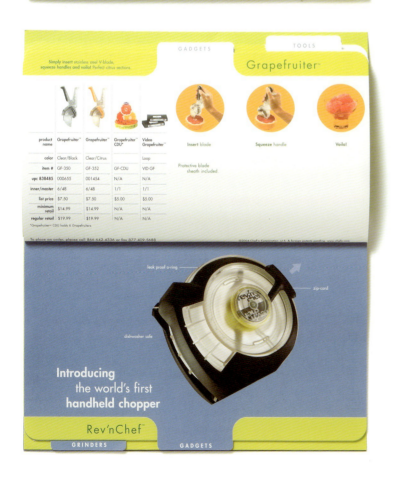

food

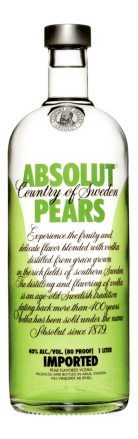

V & S Absolut Spirits
酒類製造・販売 [Alcoholic beverages maker]
DF, SB: BVD

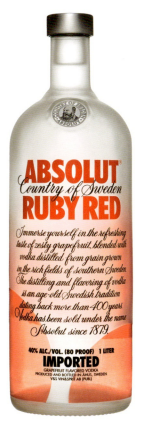

food 031

AGUAS DE FUENSANTA
ミネラルウォーターの製造・販売 [Natural spring water]
CD. AD: Pati Núñez   CD. AD. D. I: Kike Segurola
DF. SB: Pati Núñez Associats

food

和み Nagomi
お茶の製造・販売 [Tea maker]
CD, AD, D, P: 関 宙明 Hiroaki Seki　CW: フジタノリコ Noriko Fujita
I: 稲月ちほ Chiho Inatsuki　DF, SB: ミスター・ユニバース mr.universe

おいしい水の、一歩先へ。

人間は、水くさい。

キリンMC ダノンウォーターズ　KIRIN MC DANONE WATERS
非アルコール飲料製造・販売 [Nonalcoholic beverage manufacture and sales]
CD, AD, D: 佐野之美　Yukimi Sano　CD, CW: 迫田哲也　Tetsuya Sakota
D: ワタナベリツコ　Ritsuko Watanabe (Newspaper advertisement)　P: 石田 東　Higashi Ishida
I: 清川あさみ　Asami Kiyokawa　DF, SB: アサツーディ・ケイ　ASATSU-DK

新聞広告　Newspaper advertisements

food   035

新聞広告 Newspaper advertisements

サントリー SUNTORY
飲料の製造・販売 [Beverage manufacture and sales]
CD: 加藤英夫 Hideo Kato / 葛西 薫 Kaoru Kasai / 山田 健 Ken Yamada
AD, D: 岡本 学 Manabu Okamoto   I: Philippe Weisbecker
CW: 古居利康 Toshiyasu Furui / 川畑 弘 Hiroshi Kawabata
PR: 岸良真奈美 Manami Kishira / 伊比由理恵 Yurie Ibi   DF, SB: サン・アド Sun-Ad

ゆたかな香り。まろやかなコクと深み。
「いいちこパーソン」は、ひたすら磨いた
「いいちこ」のしゃれたポケットボトルです。
原料は大麦・大麦麹100%。
酵母は自慢の『蔵酵母』。
蒸溜は香りとうまみの単式蒸溜。
水は地下300mの清冽な水。
きれいな山麓の醸造場で、
ていねいに醸しました。

iichiko
PERSON
300ml Bottle
Enjoy its polished, refreshing flavor and its pure crystal clarity.

三和酒類株式会社 大分県宇佐市山本・虚空蔵寺丁
TEL.0978-32-1431 http://www.iichiko.co.jp

フルーツを想わせる香り。澄みきった深いうまみ。
「いいちこパーソン」は、ひたすら磨いた
「いいちこ」のしゃれたポケットボトルです。
原料は大麦・大麦麹100%。
酵母は自慢の『蔵酵母』。
蒸溜は香りとうまみの単式蒸溜。
水は地下300mの清冽な水。
きれいな山麓の醸造場で、
ていねいに醸しました。

iichiko
PERSON
300ml Bottle
Enjoy its polished, refreshing flavor and its pure crystal clarity.

三和酒類株式会社 大分県宇佐市山本・虚空蔵寺丁
TEL.0978-32-1431 http://www.iichiko.co.jp

038　food

ポスター　Poster

サントリー　SUNTORY
飲料の製造・販売　[Beverage manufacture and sales]
CD: 高上 晋　Shin Takaue / 玉水恭司　Kyoji Tamamizu　CD, CW: 安藤 隆　Takashi Ando　CD, AD: 葛西 薫　Kaoru Kasai
D: 宮崎 史　Fumi Miyazaki　P: 上田義彦　Yoshihiko Ueda
PR: 土井真人　Masato Doi / 小原淳平　Junpei Ohara　DF, SB: サン・アド　Sun-Ad

040 food

虎屋 Toraya Confectionery
和菓子製造・販売 [Japanese confectionery manufacture and sales]
AD: 葛西 薫 Kaoru Kasai   AD, D, I: 白井陽平 Yohei Shirai   I: 志村ふくみ Fukumi Shimura
PR: 坂東美和子 Miwako Bando / 服部彩子 Ayako Hattori / 常木宏之 Hiroyuki Tsuneki
DF, SB: サン・アド Sun-Ad

food   041

ポスター　Posters

やまこし道楽村　Yamakoshi-Doraku-Mura
地域再生コンサルタント・カフェ経営 ［Community regeneration consultant, café management］
CD: 丸山結香　Yuka Maruyama　　AD, D: 山本 敦　Atsushi Yamamoto
DF, SB: ネオス　NEOS

ランチョンマット（手すき和紙）Placemat (handmade Japanese paper)

ミニ手拭　Tenugui

042 food

ポスター Posters

JA 北魚沼 Japan Agricultural Co-operatives Kitauonuma Branch
農業協同組合 [Farming cooperative]
CD, AD, D: 権田雅彦 Masahiko Gonda
D: 小山和秋 Kazuaki Koyama / 伊東誠治 Seiji Ito / 小笠原 潤 Jun Ogasawara / 千原徹也 Tetsuya Chihara
P: 藤井 保 Tamotsu Fujii SB: P913

044　food

Tea note
紅茶及び紅茶関連雑貨の販売 [Tea and tea accessory sales]
AD, D, I: 植杉翠　Midori Uesugi
SB: Tea note

food 045

パッケージ Package

Oakville Grocery
食料雑貨店 [Grocery]
CD: David Turner & Bruce Duckworth   D, I: Shawn Rosenberger
I: John Geary   DF, SB: Turner Duckworth: London & San Francisco

 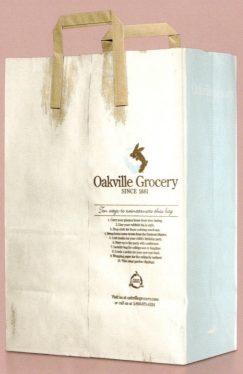

046 food

アフタヌーンティー・ティールーム　Afternoon Tea TEAROOM
飲食店 [Tea room]
[packages] CD: 古谷真希子 Makiko Furuya　D, I: 田村千穂子 Chihoko Tamura
　　　　　　AD: 澤田直子 Naoko Sawada
[butterfly & menu] CD, P: 藤原隆 Takashi Fujiwara
D: 山田亜衣子 Aiko Yamada / 遠田恭子 Yasuko Enta　I: 田村千穂子 Chihoko Tamura
SB: ビーエルティー BLT
*All staffs belong to BLT.

food   047

MOZI
通信販売 [Mail order]
SB: MOZI

food

 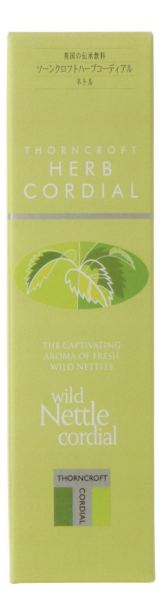 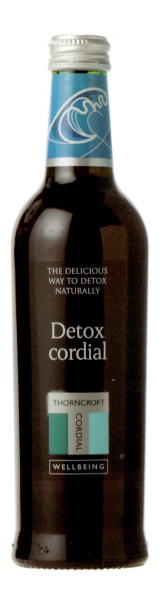 

food   049

札幌市 City of Sapporo
市町村 [City government]
AD, D: 寺島賢幸 Masayuki Terashima   DF, SB: 寺島デザイン制作室 TERASHIMA DESIGN

ソーンクロフト Thorncroft
食品製造・販売 [Food manufacture and sales]
SB: タルゴジャポン Thalgo Japon

050 food

企業組合あっぷるぴゅあ Applepure Enterprise Union
食品販売 [Food manufacture]
AD, D: 成澤豪 Go Narisawa　D, I: 成澤宏美 Hiromi Narisawa
DF, SB: なかよし図工室 Nakayoshi Zukoushitsu

名刺 Business card

シール Seals　封筒 Envelope

food 051

Jamba Juice
フルーツジュース製造・販売 [Natural fruit juice]
CD: David Turner & Bruce Duckworth
D: Tanawat Pisanuwongse / Shawn Rosenberger I: Alison Carmichael
P: Lwe Robertson (Poster & Stationery)
DF, SB: Turner Duckworth: London & San Francisco

パンフレット Pamphlet

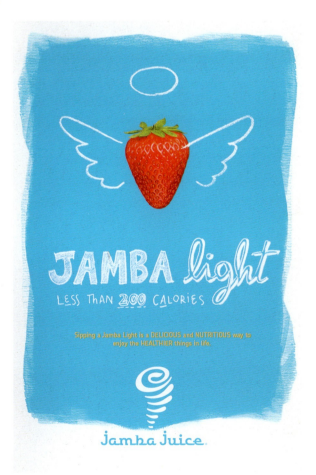

ブローシャー Brochure　　店舗マニュアル Store operation manual　　ポスター Poster

052 food

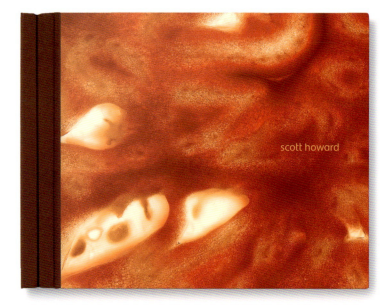

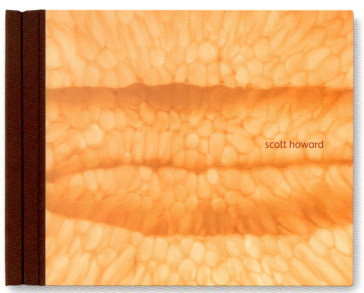
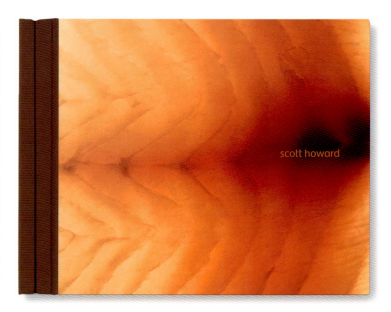

メニュー Menus

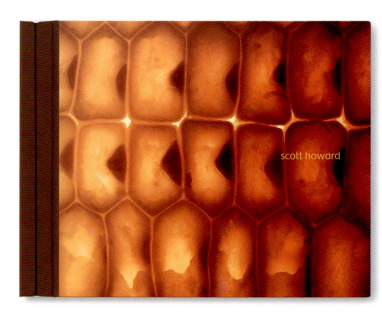

Scott Howard
レストラン [Restaurant]
CD, D: David Turner & Bruce Duckworth   P: Lloyd Hryciw
DF, SB: Turner Duckworth: London & San Francisco

food 053

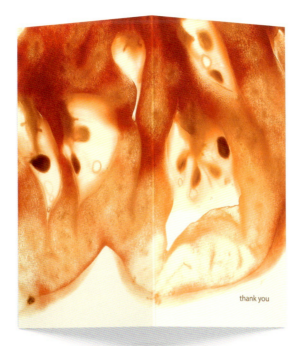

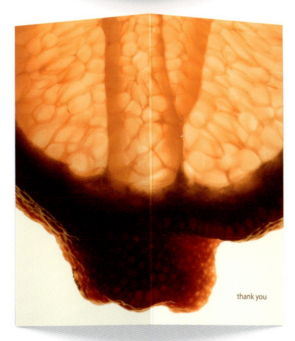

ワインリスト　Wine lists

ショップカード　Shop cards

054 food

店舗 Shop image

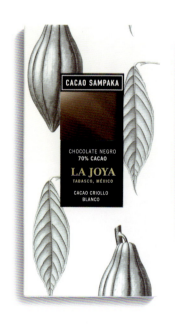

CACAO SAMPAKA
チョコレート・チェーン [Chain of Chocolate shops and factory]
CD, AD: Pati Núñez D: Esther Martin de Pozuelo P: Javier Tles DF, SB: Pati Núñez Associats

パッケージ Packages

ポスター Poster

カード Cards

コンテンポラリープランニングセンター Contemporary Planning Center
総合プロデュース・リテイル事業 [Retail-related comprehensive planning and design]
CD: 杉浦 幸 Yuki Sugiura／いがらしろみ Romi Igarashi CD, CW: 後藤国弘 Kunihiro Goto AD: 今井クミ Kumi Imai
D: 多賀健史 Takeshi Taga／小田嶋暁子 Akiko Odashima P: 新居明子 Akiko Arai Artist: 奥 まゆみ Mayumi Oku (Press kit)
DF, SB: アピスラボラトリー APIS LABORATORY

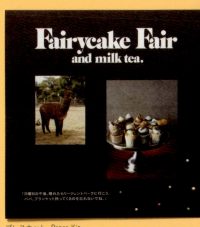

プレスキット Press Kit

ケーキボックス Cake boxes

food 057

food

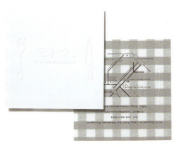
ショップカード Shop card

封筒 Envelope

メニュー Menu

ルーペ Loupe
洋菓子製造・販売 [Confectionary manufacture and sales]
AD, D: 成澤 豪 Go Narisawa　D, I: 成澤宏美 Hiromi Narisawa　P: 有賀 傑 Suguru Ariga
Artwork: 近藤佳代 Kayo Kondo　Furniture: スタンダードトレード STANDARD TRADE.
DF, SB: なかよし図工室 Nakayoshi Zukoushitsu

ピンバッジ Pin badges

060 food

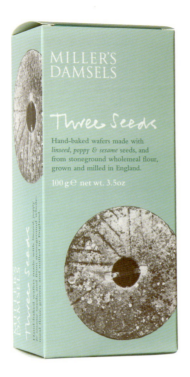

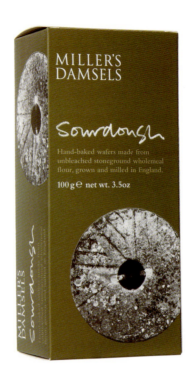
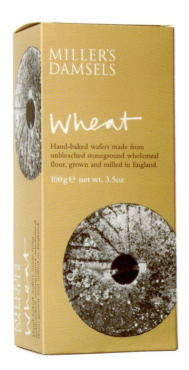

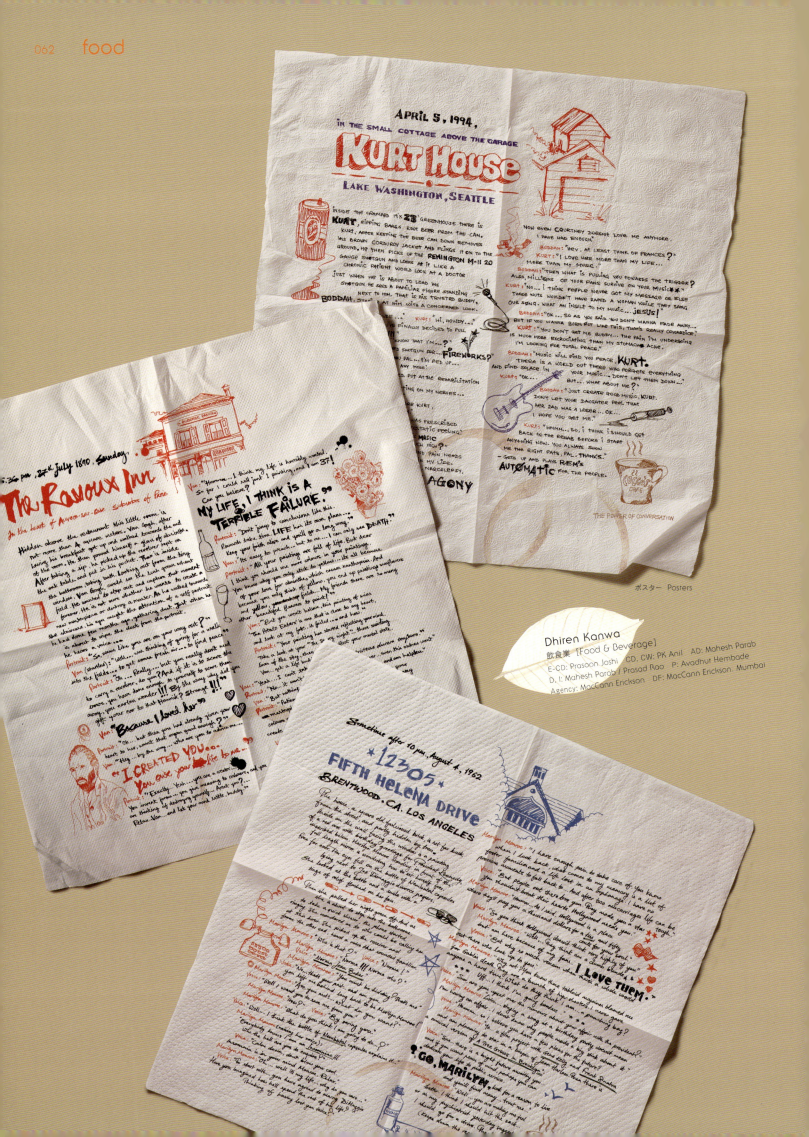

ポスター Posters

Dhiren Kanwa
飲食業 [Food & Beverage]
E-CD: Prasoon Joshi CD, CW: PK Anil AD: Mahesh Parab
D, I: Mahesh Parab / Prasad Rao P: Avadhut Hembade
Agency: MacCann Erickson DF: MacCann Erickson, Mumbai

food 063

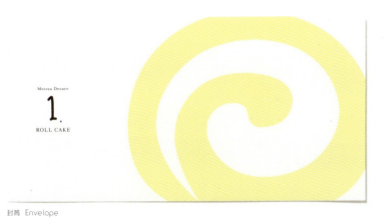

封筒 Envelope

ショップカード Shop card

ルーペ Loupe
洋菓子製造・販売 [Confectionary manufacture and sales]
AD, D: 成澤 豪 Go Narisawa   D, I: 成澤宏美 Hiromi Narisawa
DF, SB: なかよし図工室 Nakayoshi Zukoushitsu

ピンバッジ Pin badges

064 food

永井農場 NAGAI FARM
農場経営 [Farm]
AD, D, DF, SB: アトリエタイク ateliertaik

food 065

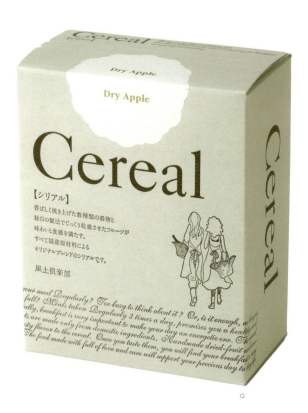

風土倶楽部 FUDOCLUB
食品販売 [Food manufacture]
AD, D: 成澤 豪 Go Narisawa　D: 成澤宏美 Hiromi Narisawa
I: 田所真理子 Mariko Tadokoro (a) / 平澤まりこ Mariko Hirasawa (b)
DF, SB: なかよし図工室 Nakayoshi Zukoushitsu

ガテモタブン Gatemo Tabum
レストラン [Restaurant]
AD, D, DF, SB: アトリエタイク ateliertaik

beauty

雑誌広告 Magazine advertisements

エキップ E'QUIPE
化粧品製造・販売 [Cosmetics]

CD: RUMIKO AD: 松田澄子 Sumiko Matsuda D: 宮澤知里 Chisato Miyazawa / 佐久間祐子 Yuko Sakuma
P: 前田洋伸 Hironobu Maeda (a, c) / 中村彰三 Shozo Nakamura (b, d, e, f)
SB: 中塚広告事務所 Nakatsuka & Partners

beauty 069

c

d

e

リーフレット　Leaflets　　f

070 beauty

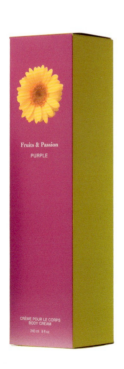

フルーツ&パッション Fruits & Passion
ビューティー&ライフスタイルブティック [Beauty & lifestyle boutique]
SB: プラザスタイル PLAZASTYLE

beauty 071

 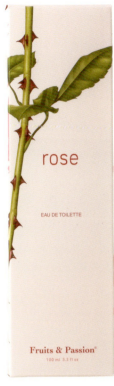    

beauty

イデアインターナショナル IDEA International
小売・卸 ［Wholesale and retail］
SB: イデアインターナショナル IDEA International
[Package] CD, AD, D: 得能正人 Masato Tokuno
D: 中田 翼 Tsubasa Nakata
[Catalog & press release] CD: 福田綾奈 Ayana Fukuda
AD, D: 植杉 翠 Midori Uesugi
[Press release folder] CD: 海渕恵理 Eri Kaifuchi
AD: 得能正人 Masato Tokuno
D: 村上知歩 Chiho Murakami

beauty 073

プレスリリース Press release

プレスリリースフォルダ Press release folder

カタログ Catalog

カタログ Catalog

beauty

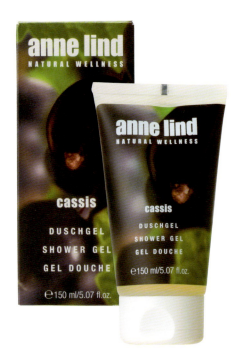
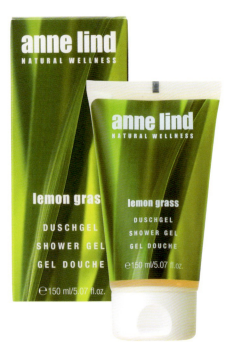
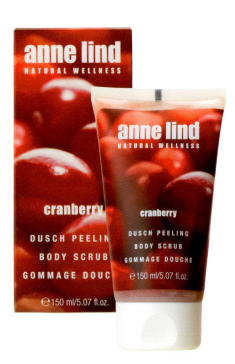

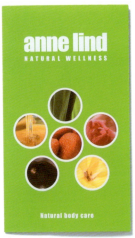

パンフレット Pamphlet

beauty 075

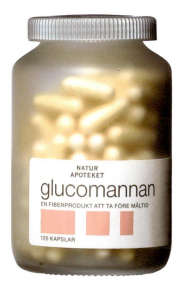

Naturapoteket
健康・美容 [Health food]
DF, SB: BVD

ピリカ インターナショナル ジャパン Pilica International Japan
化粧品輸入販売 [Cosmetics]
D: 畠山香里 Kaori Hatayama (except packages)
SB: ピリカインターナショナル Pilica International Japan

beauty

ブローシャー Brochure

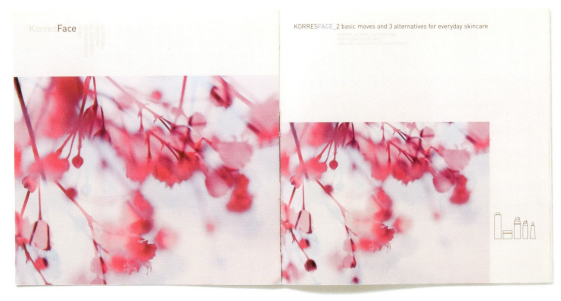

Korres Natural Products
化粧品製造・販売 [Cosmetics]
DF: k2design
SB: フィッツコーポレーション FITS Corporation

beauty 077

パッケージ Packages

店舗 Shop images

beauty

ザ・ボディショップ THE BODY SHOP
化粧品 [Cosmetics]
AD: 小松史枝 Fumie Komatsu
SB: ザ・ボディショップ THE BODY SHOP

beauty

Tahitian Noni [Retail store for health & beauty products]
健康・美容用品の小売店
[Store Design] CD: Lisa Cerveny / Sonja Max / Kathy Saito
D: Sonja Max / David Bates / Belinda Bowling / Ensi Mofasser
[Packages] CD: Lisa Cerveny / Sonja Max   D: Sonja Max / Belinda Bowling / Ensi Mofasser /
Kathy Saito / Beth Grimm / Julie Jacobson   SB: Hornall Anderson

beauty

アリエルトレーディング　Ariel Trading
輸入販売業　[Import sales]
CD: Ian Griulx (IDEO) / Joshua Onysko (PANGEA ORGANICS)
AD: Mark Woolard (IDEO)　CW: Amy Leventhal (IDEO)
D: PHil Strob (IDEO)　P. I, DF: IDEO
SB: アリエルトレーディング　Ariel Trading

beauty 081

082　beauty

ジュリーク・ジャパン　Jurlique Japan
化粧品製造・販売 ［Cosmetics］
SB: ジュリーク・ジャパン　Jurlique Japan

パンフレット Pamphlet

店舗 Shop images

beauty

薬日本堂 NIHONDO
薬局 [Pharmacy]
CD, AD, CW: 冴端雅枝 Masae kawabata　D. P. I: 堀場佳代子 Kayoko Horiba
DF: スリーミン・グラフィック・アソシエイツ 3Min. Graphic. Associates
SB: 薬日本堂 NIHONDO

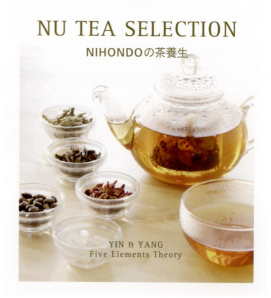

パンフレット　Pamphlet

beauty

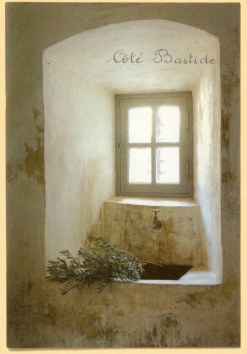

カタログ Catalog

パンフレット Japanese Pamphlet

beauty 087

カードタイプのカタログケース　Card-style catalog case

コテ・バスティド　Côté Bastide
インテリア・生活雑貨・フレグランスの製造・小売・卸販売
[Home furnishings manufacture and sales]
D: Nicol Houques　P: Henri del Olmo
Stylist: Marie Christine Caviglione
AD: Kiyomi Kizaki (Japanese Pamphlet)
SB: 林タオル フランジュール事業部　HAYASHI TOWEL FRANCJOUR DIV

088　beauty

パンフレット　Pamphlet

イグニス　IGNIS　[Cosmetics]
化粧品の製造・販売
AD: 堀切大輔　Daisuke Horikiri　P: 塚田直寛　Naohiro Tsukada
I: 野尻由起子　Yukiko Nojiri　CW: 神崎浩子　Hiroko Kanzaki
Stylist: 青木もえ　Moe Aoki　SB: アルビオン　ALBION

ポスター Posters

beauty

カタログ Catalog

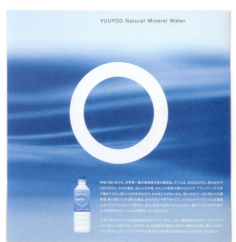

YUUYOO Organic Towels,
Woven by the Wind

ユーヨー yuuyoo
ホームコレクションブランド企画・販売 [Home collection brand planning and sales]
AD: 浅沼裕司 Yuji Asanuma　I: 佐藤正樹 Masaki Sato
SB: インナチュラル IN NATURAL

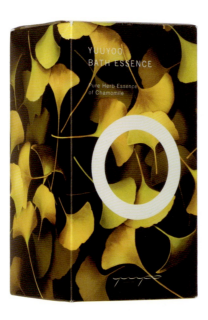
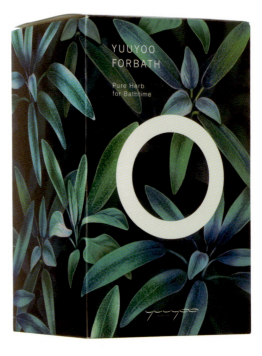

beauty 091

新聞広告 Newspaper advertisements

資生堂 SHISEIDO
化粧品製造・販売 [Cosmetics]
D, SB: 月岡正明 Masaaki Tsukioka　D: 中原早季 Saki Nakahara
P: 助田徹臣 Tetsuomi Sukeda

092　beauty

IDESA PARFUMS
香水製造・広告 [Perfume creation and commercialization]
CD, AD: Pati Núñez　D: Esther Martin de Pozuelo
P: Alexis Taule (Lovely Blossom) / Takushi Katafuchi (In Red)
DF, SB: Pati Núñez Associats

パッケージ　Package

Liz Earle Cosmetics
化粧品製造・販売 [Naturally Active Skincare]
CD: David Turner & Bruce Duckworth   D: Bruce Duckworth (Skin care) / Jamie McCathie (Gift Packages)
Retouching, Artwork: Neil MacCall   DF, SB: Turner Duckworth: London & San Francisco

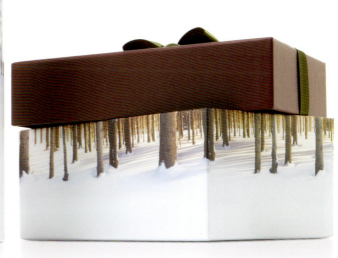

ギフトパッケージ　Gift Packages

パンフレット　Pamphlets

beauty

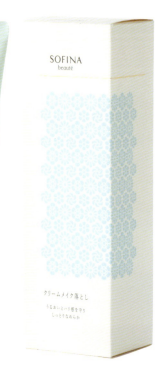

花王 Kao Corporation
化粧品製造・販売 [Cosmetics]
CD: 宮田 識 Satoru Miyata / 石井昌彦 Masahiko Ishii   AD: 渡邉良重 Yoshie Watanabe
D: 前原翔一 Shoichi Maehara / 秋山保子 Yasuko Akiyama   I: 宇那手有子 Yuko Unate
P: 和田 恵 Megumu Wada (ドアブル Doable) / 矢島由香 Yuka Yajima / 小宮由美子 Yumiko Komiya
CW: 渡辺恵里子 Eriko Watanabe
DF: 博報堂 Hakuhodo / ドラフト Draft   SB: 花王 Kao Corporation

リーフレット Leaflet

beauty 095

Sainsbury's plc
スーパーマーケット・小売 [Supermarket and retailer]
D: Paul Cartwright   P: Carol Sharp Photography
DF, SB: Paul Cartwright Branding

玉の肌石鹸 TAMANOHADA
化粧石鹸・シャンプー・コンディショナーなどの
製造販売・研究開発
[Personal care products R&D, manufacture and sales]
D: 西村理恵 Rie Nishimura   CW: 後藤国弘 Kunihiro Goto
DF, SB: 玉の肌石鹸 TAMANOHADA

a

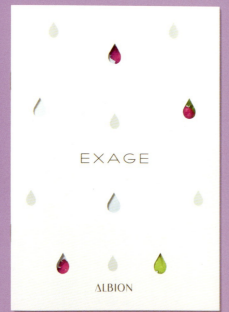

b

アルビオン ALBION
化粧品製造・販売 [Cosmetics]
AD: 沢田孝子 Takako Sawada
D: 沢田孝子 Takako Sawada (c, d, e, f) / 多賀久子 Hisako Taga (a, b)
P: 横浪 修 Osamu Yokonami (a) / 新倉哲也 Tetsuya Niikura (b) /
皆倉 亮 Ryo Kaikura (c, d, e) / 内山拓也 Takuya Uchiyama (f)
CW: 下地千晴 Chiharu Shimoji (a) / 橋口奈苗 Nanae Hashiguchi (c, d, e)
SB: アルビオン ALBION

beauty 097

c

d

e f

098 beauty

JILL by JILLSTUART
デザイナーズブランド [Designer brand]
P.R.Director: 山田初美 Hatsumi Yamada (Smile inc.)   AD. CD. D: 近藤麻由 Mayu Kondo (The VOICE)
P: Andrew Durham   Stylist: Shun Watanabe (STIJL)   Hair: Tony Chavez
Make up: Yumi   Models: Sonja Kinski / Alexandra Richards   Production: HK productions
Local Producer: Christine Clayton   SB: サンエー・インターナショナル SANEI-INTERNATIONAL

beauty 099

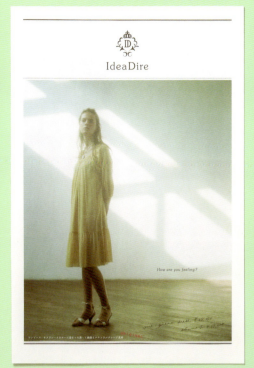
カタログ Catalog

ショップバッグ Shop bags

ワールド WORLD
婦人・紳士・子供服の企画・販売 [Men's, women's and children's clothing]
AD: 池田泰幸 Yasuyuki Ikeda D: 西村美博 Yoshihiro Nishimura / 土屋絵里子 Eriko Tsuchiya
P: 山根範久 Norihisa Yamane CW: 小宮由美子 Yumiko Komiya
PR: 岸良真奈美 Manami Kishira / 上野 敬 Kei Ueno DF, SB: サン・アド Sun-Ad

beauty

ポイント Point
アパレル [Apparel]
AD, D: 青木康子 Yasuko Aoki
Shop design: 李 明喜 Myeong-hee Lee
DF, SB: PANGAEA

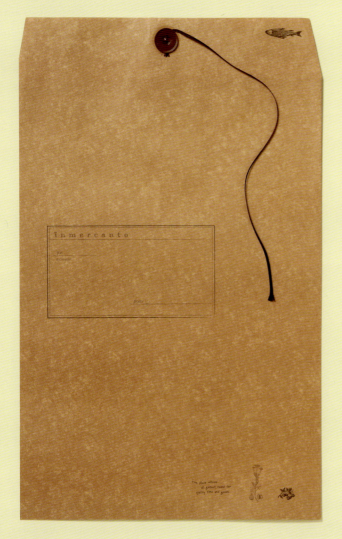

ショップツール Shop tools

beauty 101

FRAME WORKS
アパレル [Apparel]
AD, SB: 大島依提亜 Idea Oshima　P: 端 裕人 Hiroto Hata
Stylist: 柳田真樹 Maki Yanagida　Hair & Make: JIRO for Kilico

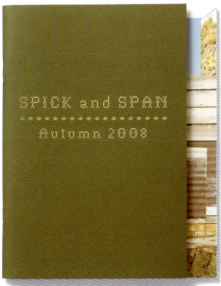

カタログ　Catalog

beauty

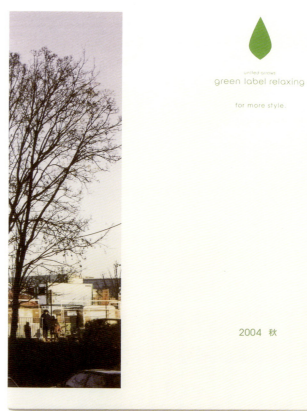

ユナイテッドアローズ UNITED ARROWS
アパレル及び雑貨等の企画・販売 [Apparel and novelties manufacture and sales]
CD, CW: 笠原千晶 Chiaki Kasahara　AD, D: 今井クミ Kumi Imai　P: 新津保健秀 Kenshu Shintsubo
PR: 徳永あかね Akane Tokunaga　DF, SB: アピスラボラトリー APIS LABORATORY

beauty 103

シーズンブック Season book (2008-2009Autumn/Winter collection)

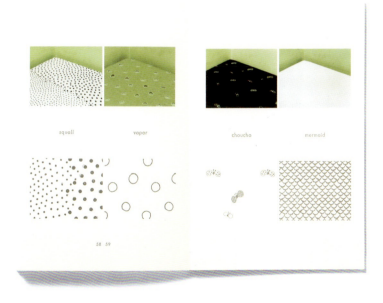

ポストカード Post card

ミナ ペルホネン minä perhonen
ファッションブランド [Fashon brand]
SB: ミナ ペルホネン minä perhonen   DF: PLUG-IN GRAPHIC   P: 戎 康友 Yasutomo Ebisu
[Season book] AD: 平林奈緒美 Naomi Hirabayashi   Hair Make: 茅根裕己 Hiromi Chinone (Cirque)
Stylist: 岡尾美代子 Miyoko Okao
[Post card] D: 名久井直子 Naoko Nakui   P: 竹原麻希子 Makiko Takehara

©minä perhonen

beauty

ジャーナル スタンダード ラックス journal standard luxe
アパレル [Apparel]
AD, D: 平林奈緒美 Naomi Hirabayashi P: 戎 康友 Yasutomo Ebisu
DF: PLUG-IN GRAPHIC Styling: journal standard luxe
Hair Make: 茅根裕己 Hiromi Chinone SB: JS.WORKS

Image book

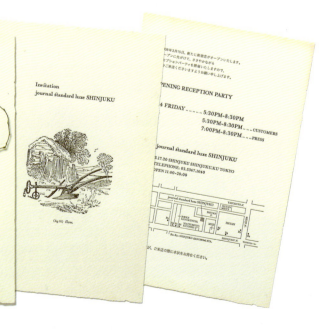

Invitation

ヨーガンレール Jurgen Lehl
デザイナーズブランド [Designer brand]
AD: 松浦秀昭 Hideaki Matsuura D: ヨーガンレール Jurgen Lehl

季節DM Seasonal invitation

パルコ PARCO
百貨店 〔Department store〕
CD. CW: パルコ PARCO   CD. AD. D. I. CW: 板倉敬子 Keiko Itakura
P: 市橋織江 Orie Ichihashi   DF. SB: イッカクイッカ Ikkakuikka

beauty 107

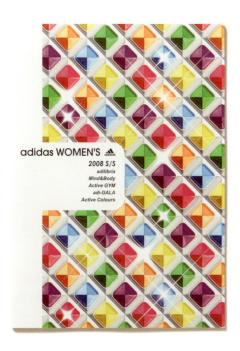

AVEDA
化粧品製造・販売 [Cosmetics]
AD, D: 近藤麻由 Mayu Kondo
DF, SB: ザ・ボイス The VOICE

アディダス ジャパン adidas japan
スポーツ用品アパレル [Sportswear]
AD: 山口アツシ Atsushi Yamaguchi
DF, SB: スーパーミー Super me

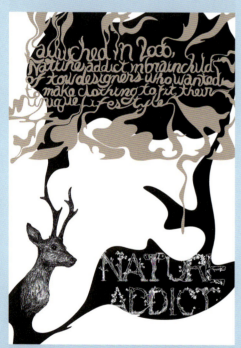

ポスター Posters

ネイチャー アディクト NATURE ADDICT
アパレル [Apparel]
AD, D, I, Artwork, SB: 大黒大悟 Daigo Daikoku

beauty 109

ポスター Posters

ウォームプロジェクト　WARM PROJECT
テキスタイル [Textiles]
AD, D, I, Artwork, SB: 大黒大悟　Daigo Daikoku

110 beauty

beauty 111

グリュック glück
美容室 [Beauty salon]
CD, AD: 新ヶ江友也 Tomoya Shingae　AD, D: 熊谷由紀 Yuki Kumagae
P: 進藤祐光 Yuko Shindo　CW: 忽那久子 Hisako Kotsuna

ポスター Posters

ポスター Poster

ビューティー・ソノ Beauty Sono
美容室 [Beauty salon]
AD, D: 上平穏人 Minoru Uehira
DF, SB: 上平穏人デザイン室 Minoru Uehira Design Office

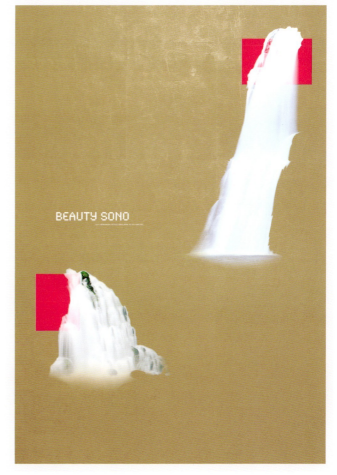

ギャラリー レタ gallery LETA
ハンドメイドショップ [Handicraft shop]
AD, D, I, SB: 大黒大悟 Daigo Daikoku

ポスター Posters

beauty

ポスター Posters

ポスター Poster

美容室アイリス Hair salon Irys
美容室 [Beauty salon]
AD, D: 坂本尚美 Naomi Sakamoto DF, SB: E

エム 美容室 Hair Salon "M"
美容室 [Beauty salon]
AD, D: 森 雅代 Masaya Mori
DF, SB: 寺島デザイン制作室 TERASHIMA DESIGN

beauty   115

ポスター Poster

名刺 Business card

金券 Tickets

こころ Kokoro
リラクゼーションサロン [Relaxation salon]
AD, D: 目谷裕美子 Yumiko Meya　CW, Typographer: 杉田真理 Mari Sugita
DF, SB: キンザ座 Kinzaza

ショップカード Shop Card

チラシ Flyer

ポスター Poster

home 119

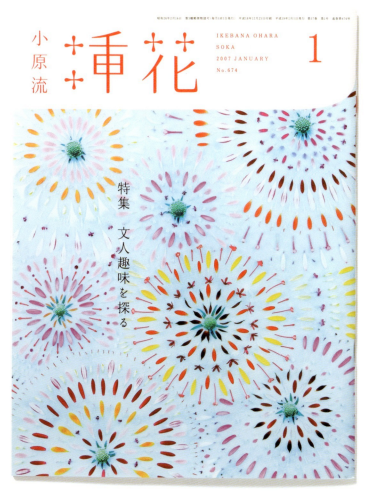

小原流 OHARA SCHOOL of IKEBANA
生け花の学校 [School of Ikebana]
AD: 永田武史 Takeshi Nagata　D: 鹿島絵美 Emi Kashima / 田代奈々 Nana Tashiro
P: 中島宏樹 Hiroki Nakashima　Stylist: 青木もえ Moe Aoki
SB: エヌ・デザイン enudesign

雑誌 Magazines

NISSANは、車内外クリーンエア

「クルマの外の空気も、中の空気も、気持ちよく」が、NISSANのテーマ。

車外は、燃費を向上させてCO_2排出を抑えるとともに、

排出ガスのクリーン化やクルマの電動化などの技術開発を進めています。

車内は、空気を自動的にきれいにしたり、

体への負担を軽減するなど、より快適な室内環境を実現します。

最新の成果として、まず、燃費を向上させた新エンジンと

インテリジェントエアコンシステムを搭載したコンパクトカー6車種が登場しました。

私たちは「NISSAN GREEN PROGRAM 2010」に基づき、

環境に対して独自の取り組みを進めています。

www.nissan.co.jp/ECO

PIVO
「人を中心においた技術革新」を
象徴するNISSANの
電気自動車（コンセプトカー）です。

 SHIFT_eco

雑誌広告 Magazine advertisement

カレンダー Calendar

パルス BALS
リテール・プロダクツ・スペースクリエイション [Retail, Products, Space creation]
AD: 富田光浩 Mitsuhiro Tomita   PR: 中岡美奈子 Minako Nakaoka
DF. SB: ドラフト DRAFT

日産自動車 NISSAN MOTOR
運輸 [Transport]
CD: 松井美樹 Miki Matsui   AD: 永井一史 Kazufumi Nagai   D: 高嶋紀男 Norio Takashima   I. DF: 博報堂デザイン HAKUHODO DESIGN
P: 中島宏樹 Hiroki Nakashima   CW: 木村 透 Toru Kimura
SB: TBWA 博報堂 TBWA HAKUHODO

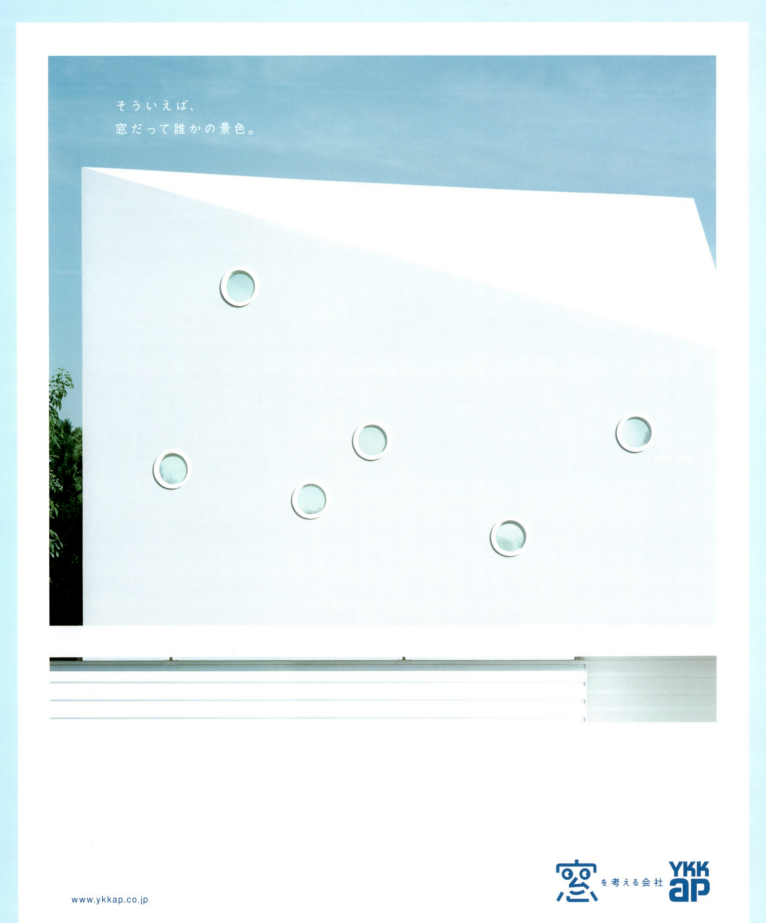

home

YKK AP
住宅・ビル建材 [Building materials]
CD: 町田聖二 Seiji Machida / 浜島達也 Tatsuya Hamajima
AD: 宮下良介 Ryosuke Miyashita D: 飯島信幸 Nobuyuki Iijima / 後藤和也 Kazuya goto
Art Work: 吉嶺直樹 Naoki Yoshimine (a) / 小林康秀 Yasuhide Kobayashi
P: 舛本晋一 Shinichi Masumoto Retouch: 桜井素直 Sunao Sakurai (a, b, c) / 山本貴幸 Takayuki Yamamoto (d) Stylist: 青木もえ Moe Aoki CW: 中里耕平 Kohei Nakazato / 高橋大 Masaru Takahashi
PR: 加藤秀人 Hidero Kato / 大塚としえ Toshie Otsuka
SB: ビルド・クリエイティブハウス BUILD creativehaus

124 home

Shaklee
栄養・健康に関する製品 [Nutrition / Wellness]
CD: David Turner & Bruce Duckworth   D: Shawn Rosenberger
P, I: Danny Smithe   DF, SB: Turner Duckworth: London & San Francisco

イケヤ IKEYA
キッズコーナー企画・運営・販売等 [Children's corner planning, operations, retail]
AD: 富田光浩 Mitsuhiro Tomita   CW: 蛭田瑞穂 Mizuho Hiruta   I: 大塚いちお Ichio Otsuka
PR: 中岡美奈子 Minako Nakaoka   DF, SB: ドラフト DRAFT

ブランドブック Brand book

home

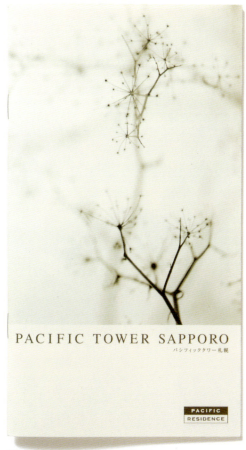

パンフレット　Pamphlet

リーフレット　Leaflet

ポスター Posters

リクルート RECRUIT
ウェブサイト運営等 [Website management]
AD: 永田武史 Takeshi Nagata　D, CW: 林 康章 Yasuaki Hayashi
D: 鹿島絵美 Emi Kashima / 佐藤亮平 Ryohei Sato / 田向井 潤 Jun Tamukai
Stylist: 青木むすび Musubi Aoki　P: 中島宏樹 Hiroki Nakashima
SB: エヌ・デザイン enudesign

都市デザインシステム URBAN DESIGN SYSTEM
不動産 [Real estate]
CD, CW: 所 俊彦 Toshihiko Tokoro　AD, D: 上田 亮 Ryo Ueda　P: 古瀬 桂 Katsura Furuse
Printing Director: 武田 清 Kiyoshi Takeda　Stylist: 安藤 恵 Megumi Ando
DF, SB: コミューン COMMUNE

128　home

メルクロス　MERCROS Corporation
インテリア雑貨メーカー　[Home accessories manufacture]
SB: メルクロス　MERCROS Corporation

home 129

ポスター Posters

リーフレット Leaflet

DM

下甚商店 Shimojin
家具製造・販売 [Furniture manufacture and sales]
CD, AD, D, P: 関 宙明 Hiroaki Seki D: 溝川なつ美 Natsumi Mizokawa
CW: フジタノリコ Noriko Fujita I: 庄野ナホコ Nahoko Shono
DF, SB: ミスター・ユニバース mr.universe

home

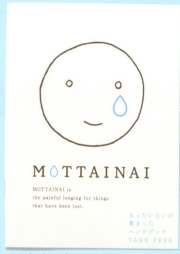

コンセプトブック Concept book

伊藤忠商事 ITOCHU Corporation / 毎日新聞社 MAINICHI NEWSPAPERS
商社／新聞社 [Trading / Newspaper] MOTTAINAI キャンペーン MOTTAINAI Campaign
I: 寄藤文平 Bunpei Yorifuji (except furoshiki) Production: スプーン Spoon SB: MOTTAINAI キャンペーン P: 金玖美 Koomi Kim
[Concept book] AD: 中村圭介 Keisuke Nakamura D: 小酒井祥悟 Shogo Kosakai (ナカムラグラフ nakamuragraph) / 鮫島雄一 Yuichi Samejima (イーター Eater)
Editor: 柴田貴寛 Takahiro Shibata (イーター Eater) / 呉屋秀樹 Hideki Goya (イーター Eater) Display Direction: 山下真太郎 Shintaro Yamashita
[T-Shirt] D: セキユリヲ Yurio Seki [Furoshiki] D: 前内道彦 Michihiko Yanai [Shop] D: ラブザライフ love the life

店舗 Shop image

home 131

フロシキ Furoshiki

新聞広告 Newspaper advertisements

ダイキン工業 DAIKIN INDUSTORIES
電機 [Home and industrial appliances]
CD: 田中 博 Hiroshi Tanaka AD: 宮田央久 Fumihisa Miyata D: 後藤恵美子 Emiko Goto / 奥野寛幸 Hiroyuki Okuno
PL: 山中貴裕 Takahiro Yamanaka / 白井友博 Tomohiro Shirai / 治部 央 Hisashi Harube / 枡田武志 Takeshi Masuda
CW: 山中貴裕 Takahiro Yamanaka DF: 大広 Daiko / 協愛 Kyoai SB: ダイキン工業 DAIKIN INDUSTORIES

134 home

新聞広告 Newspaper advertisements　　a　　　　　　　　　　　　　　　　　　　　　　　b

新聞広告 Newspaper advertisement　　e　　　　　　　　　雑誌広告 Magazine advertisements　　f

住友林業 SUMITOMO FORESTRY
総合住生活関連事業 [General housing and lifestyle-related business]

ポスター Posters

パイオニア Pioneer
音響機器・映像機器の製造・販売 [Audio-visual electronics manufacture and sales]
CA: TUGBOAT / TUGBOAT2 CD: TUGBOAT AD: 加藤建吾 Kengo Kato 新井 崇 Takashi Arai / 山田靖子 Yasuko Yamada
CW: 道面宣久 Norihisa Dohmen D: 竹中智博 Tomohiro Takenaka PM: 溝渕浩司 Koji Mizobuchi
P: 瀧本幹也 Mikiya Takimoto PR: 谷口宏幸 Hiroyuki Taniguchi PM: 溝渕浩司 Koji Mizobuchi
Supervisor: 仙波 修 Osamu Senba DF: アサツーディ・ケイ ASATSU-DK / TUGBOAT SB: TUGBOAT2

東京オペラシティアートギャラリー Tokyo Opera City Art Gallery
美術館 [Museum]
AD, SB: 大島依提亜 Idea Oshima P: 高橋ヨーコ Yoko Takahashi
Stylist: 岡尾美代子 Miyoko Okao

チケット Tikets

ポスター Poster

Schumacher
織物・壁紙の販売 [Textiles and wallcoverings]
CD: Bill Sorrell D, SB: Lizette Gecel I: Ultimate Symbol
DF: The Sorrell Company

パンフレット Pamphlet

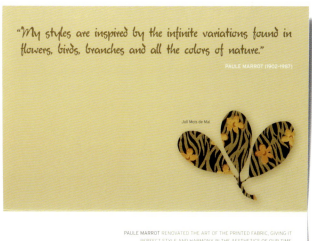

140　home

雑誌　Magazines

草月出版　Sogetsu Shuppan
いけばな流派・出版　[School of Ikebana / Publishing]
AD, D, SB: 佐藤晃一　Koichi Sato

昭文社　Shobunsha Publications
出版・電子地図　[Publishing / Digital maps]
D: 金内由紀江　Yukie Kamauchi　DF: グリッド　Grid
SB: 昭文社　Shobunsha Publications

home   141

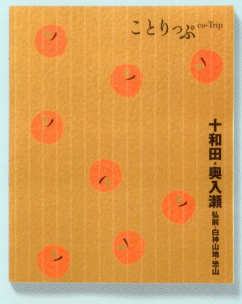

装丁 Book covers

リーフレット　Leaflets

中央出版 アノニマスタジオ anonima st.
出版 [Publishing]
CD, AD: 関 宙明 Hiroaki Seki　D: 溝川なつ美 Natsumi Mizokawa
I: 松尾ミユキ Miyuki Matsuo / 伊藤絵理子 Eriko Ito / 得地直美 Naomi Tokuchi / 森 千章 Chiaki Mori / 北村範史 Norichika Kitamura
DF, SB: ミスター・ユニバース mr.universe

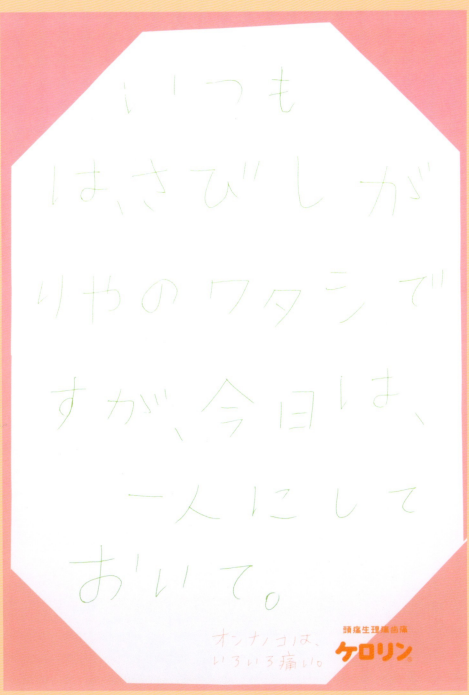

ポスター　Posters

内外薬品　Naigai Yakuhin
製薬 [Pharmaceuticals]
CD, CW: 高橋修宏　Nobuhiro Takahashi　AD, D, SB: 宮田裕美詠　Yumiyo Miyata
DF: クロス　CROSS / ストライド　STRIDE

home

ポスター　Posters

ブローシャー　Brochure

home 145

リビングデザインセンター Living Design Center
展示・催しの企画・運営等 [Exhibition / rental gallery management]
AD, D, DF, SB: アトリエタイク atelierraik

AGUAYO & HEUBENER
不動産 [Real estate marketing]
CD, D: Julia Vakser / Matthew Anderson   D: Jonathan Corriera
DF: Hyperakt Design Group   Principal: Deroy Peraza
PM: Rosemary Hahn   SB: Hyperakt

146 home

イベントカレンダー Events Calendar

home   147

Brooklyn Bridge Park Conservancy
NPO 法人 [NPO]   I: Park Renderings: Michael Van Valkenburgh Associates
CD, D: Jonathan Goldberg   D: Deroy Peraza   PM: Rosemary Hahn   SB: Hyperakt
DF: Hyperakt Design Group   Principal: Deroy Peraza

Fabryo Corp.
染料 [Dyes & paints]   DF, SB: Brandient
CD: Cristian Kit Paul   D: Alin Tamasan

148 home

ポスター Posters

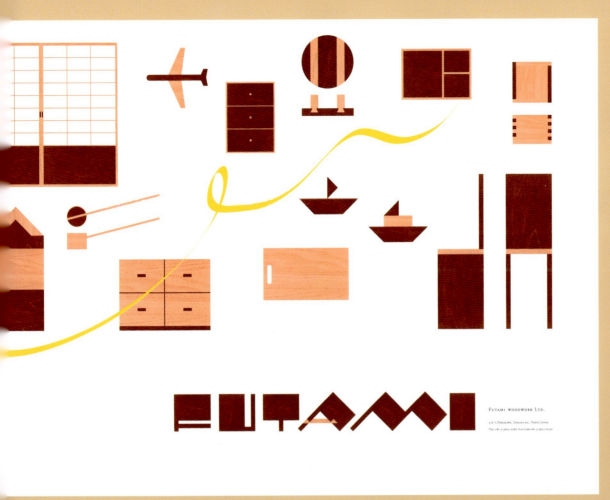
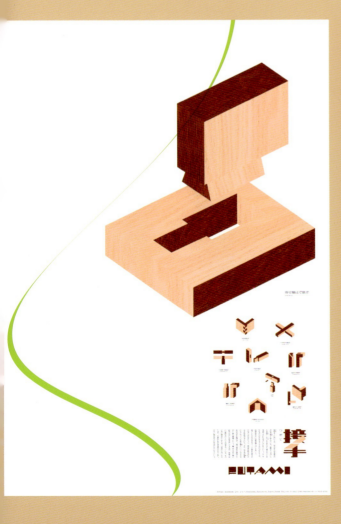

富民木工 FUTAMI Woodwork
建具施工［Joinery］
AD, D: 上平稔人 Minoru Uehira　DF, SB: 上平稔人デザイン室 Minoru Uehira Design office

home 150

ポスター Posters

リーフレット Leaflet

シュロ SyuRo
小物・雑貨の製造・販売 [Novelties manufacture and sales]
CD, AD, P: 関 宙明 Hiroaki Seki　D: 溝川なつ美 Natsumi Mizokawa
CW: 忽那久子 Hisako Kotsuna　DF, SB: ミスター・ユニバース mr.universe

home   151

招待状 Invitation

Electrolux Floor Care and Light Appliances
家電メーカー [Home electric appliances maker]
DF, SB: BVD

Green Genes
子ども服・小物ブティック
[Eco-friendly boutique specializing in green goodies for children]
D: Eric Kass   DF, SB: Funnel: Eric Kass: Utilitarian + Commercial + Fine: Art

home

DELPHINE
文具・カード制作・販売 [Stationary & Invitations]
CD, AD, D, I: Erika Firm
DF, SB: DELPHINE

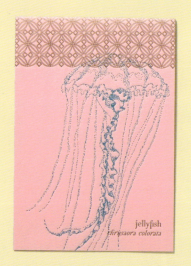
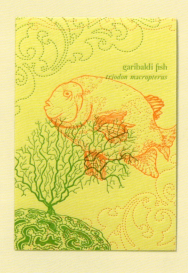

home 153

ポストカード Post cards

デポ Des Pots
製造業 [Manufacturing]
CD: いがらしろみ Romi Igarashi　　D: 茂木隆行 Takayuki Motegi　　P: 公文美和 Miwa Kumon
CW: 赤澤かおり Kaori Akazawa　　SB: デポ Des Pots

エコトワザ Ecotwaza
環境サービス業 [Eco-friendly services]
AD, D: 長澤昌彦 Masahiko Nagasawa　CW: 岡田健一 Kenichi Okada / 大塚玲奈 Reina Otsuka
I: 天本恵子 Keiko Amamoto　SB: マヒコ Mahiko

パンフレット Pamplet

others 159

DM

DM

入場チケット Tickets

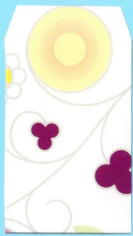

ノベルティ Novelties

others 160

ポスター Posters

草子舎 Sosisha
出版 [Publishing]
CD: 高橋修宏 Nobuhiro Takahashi　AD, D, SB: 宮田裕美詠 Yumiyo Miyata
CW: 鈴木六林男 Murio Suzuki (Haiku)　DF: ストライド STRIDE

ポスター Posters

川村記念美術館 Kawamura Memorial Museum of Art
美術館 [Museum]
AD: 永井裕明 Hiroaki Nagai　D: 高橋かおる Kaoru Takahashi
P: 長沢慎一郎 Shinichiro Nagasawa　DF, SB: エヌ・ジー N.G

なかよし図工室展

期間 二〇〇四年 一一月一七日(水)〜一二月九日(木)
場所 紅茶舗 葉々屋 Tea Room
時間【shop】一一時〇〇〜一九時〇〇/【Tea Room】一一時三〇〜一九時〇〇 年中無休（冬季休暇あり）
http://www.yoyoya.com/

なかよしミトン

さむいさむい冬の朝。
朝食でいただくミルクティーは、いつも葉々屋のディンブラ No.18。
少し甘めに淹れたミルクティーとハイジの白パンを、ふっくりとほおばるとき、
白いブラインド越しの、朝の木漏れ日と出会ったような、
やわらかであたたかい仕合わせを感じるのです。
来る日も、来る日もいただくミルクティーとパン。
山のようになる茶葉の出がらしからは、静にゆげがたゆたうキッチン。
日々の暮らしの中で、毎日おとずれる、とても静かなはじまり。
"普段通り。という幸せを、いつもの白パンと葉々屋のミルクティーが運んでくれるのです。
そんなやわらかであたたかな仕合わせのしくみを
パンのようにふわふわのミトンの手袋にたくしました。

others 163

資生堂 Shiseido
化粧品メーカー [Cosmetics]
AD, D: 青木康子 Yasuko Aoki　DF, SB: PANGAEA

展覧会DM　Exhibition DM

展覧会カタログ　Exhibition catalog

なかよし図工室 Nakayoshi Zukoushitsu
デザイン会社 [Design Firm]
AD, D: 成澤 豪 Go Narisawa　D: 成澤宏美 Hiromi Narisawa
DF, SB: なかよし図工室 Nakayoshi Zukoushitsu

others

カタログ Catalog

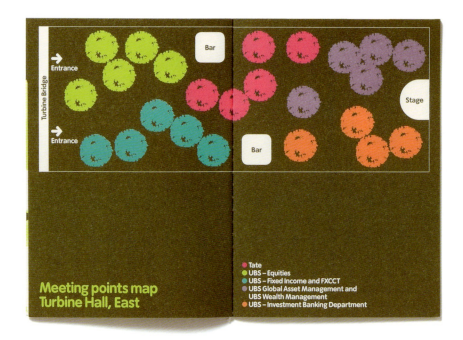

UBS / Tate
銀行・アートギャラリー [Bank / Art gallery]
CD: Warren Beeby / Phil Evans
SB: BB/Saunders

封筒 Envelope

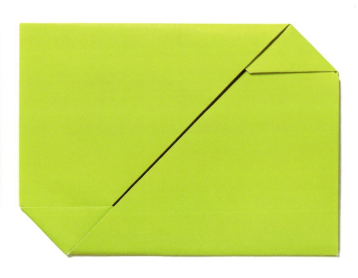

others 165

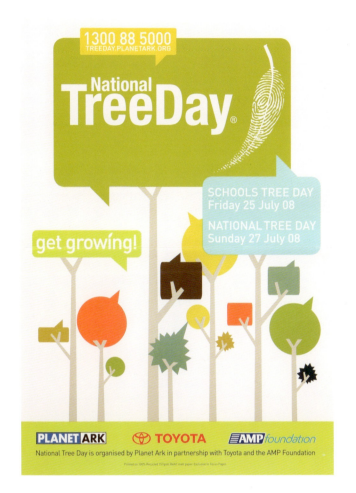

Planetark
NGO 団体 [NGO]
CD: Steven Joseph   D, I: Leah Procko   DF, SB: SPATCHURST

パンフレット Pamphlet

ポスター Poster

NATURMUSEUM SÜTIROL
自然博物館 [Museum of Nature]
CD, D: Philipp Putzer   AD: Alfons Demetz
P: Tappeiner   SB: Gruppe Gut

2005年日本国際博覧会協会 Organizing Committee for the EXPO 2005
財団法人 [Organization]
AD: 三木 健 Ken Miki　D: 酒井田成之 Shigeyuki Sakaida
DF, SB: 三木 健デザイン事務所 Ken Miki & Associates

others

三井住友フィナンシャルグループ Sumitomo Mitsui Financial Group
金融 [Finance]
CD: 石川 透 Tohru Ishikawa   AD: 山本和弘 Kazuhiro Yamamoto
D: 入江 浩 Hiroshi Irie / 伊藤健介 Kensuke Ito   DF, SB: ビルド・クリエイティブハウス BUILD creativehaus
CW: 玉山貴康 Takayasu Tamayama   DF, SB: ビルド・クリエイティブハウス BUILD creativehaus
DF: 電通 DENTSU / たき工房 TAKI CORPORATION

パッケージ Packages

Smartree
IT・ソフトウェア [IT and software]
CD, P: Cristian Kit Paul   DF, SB: Brandient

168　others

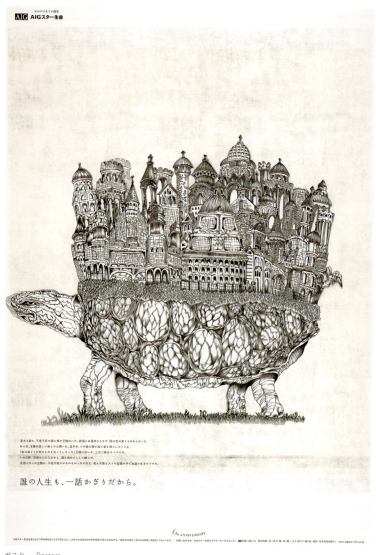

ポスター　Posters

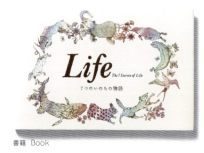

書籍　Book

AIGスター生命保険　A Member of American International Group
生命保険 [Insurance]
CD, AD: 梅谷健司 Kenji Umetani　D: 渡辺希望 Nozomu Watanabe / 上杉麻美 Asami Uesugi
I: mashi　CW: 松田 健 Ken Matsuda　PR: 加藤貴治 Takaharu Kato
Agency, SB: アサツーディ・ケイ ASATSU-DK　DF: スウィッシュ＆センシャス swish & sensuous

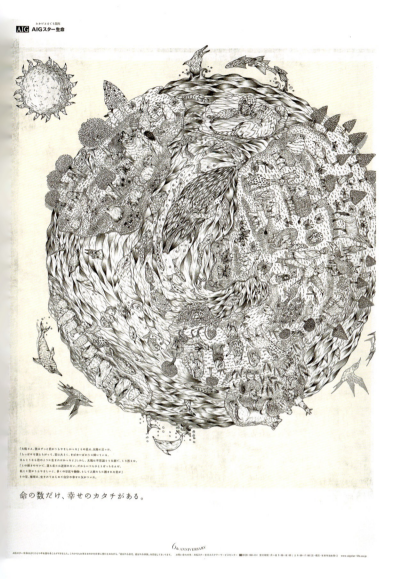

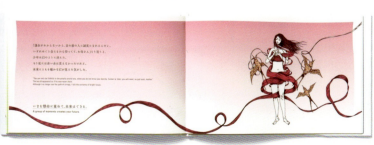

170 others

a

b

ロイヤルオークリゾート ROYAL OAK RESORT
ホテル経営 [Hotel management]
CD, AD, D: 今井クミ Kumi Imai
D: 金子朋世 Tomoyo Kaneko (a) / 多賀健史 Takeshi Taga / 橋詰千春 Chiharu Hashizume (a) / 小田嶋暁子 Akiko Odashima (a)
P: 森 雅美 Masami Mori CW: 遠藤真由美 Mayumi Endo DF, SB: アピスラボラトリー APIS LABORATORY

others

パンフレット　Pamphlet

高知県四万十町　Kochi Shimanto Town
市町村　[Local government]
CD: 樋口正仁　Masahito Higuchi　AD: 野中大樹　Taiki Nonaka
D, CW: 高橋裕子　Yuko Takahashi　P: 大石敬之　Hiroyuki Oishi
DF, SB: メディア・エーシー　Media AC

リビングデザインセンター　Living Design Center
展示・催しの企画・運営等　[Exhibition / rental gallery management]
AD, D, SB: アトリエタイク　ateliertaik　Agent: トランク　TRUNK
Producer: 桐山登士樹　Toshiki Kiriyama

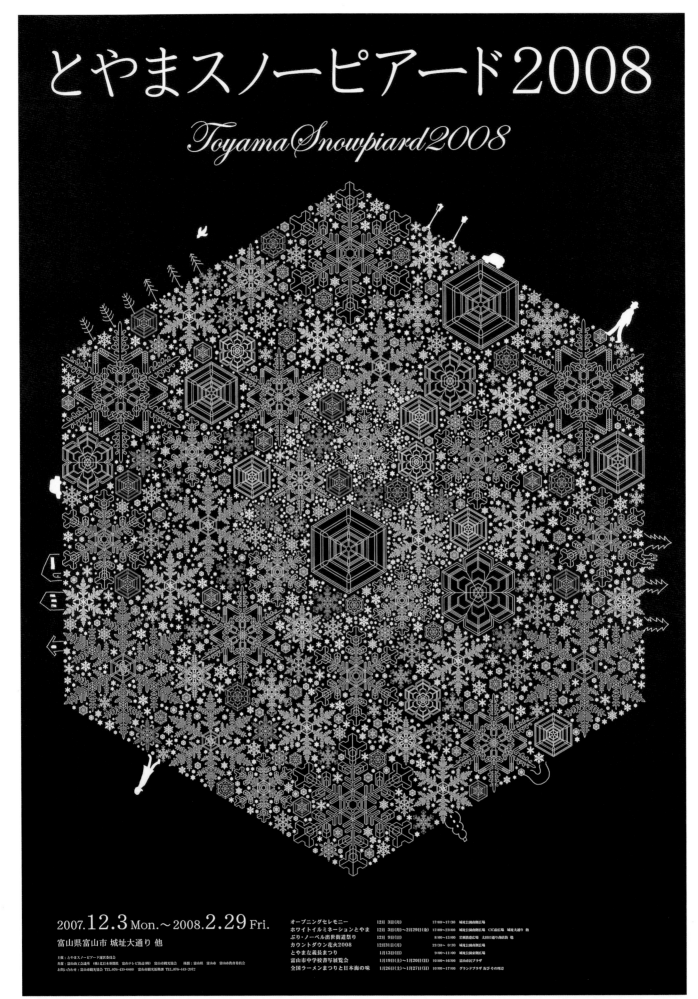
ポスター Poster

others 173

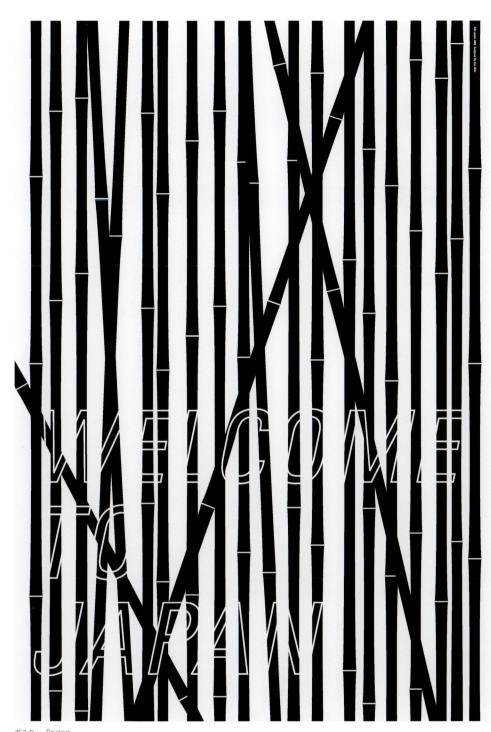

ポスター Posters

国際グラフィック連盟 Alliance Graphique Internationale Japan
デザイン団体 [Design association]
CD, AD: 三木 健 Ken Miki
DF, SB: 三木 健デザイン事務所 Ken Miki & Associates

とやまスノーピアード運営委員会
Toyama Snowpiard Steering Committee
地方自治体のイベント運営 [Local government events management]
AD, D, SB: 宮田裕美詠 Yumiyo Miyata   D: 松田良子 Ryoko Matsuda   DF: ストライド STRIDE

ポスター Poster

DM

水戸芸術振興財団 Mito Arts Foundation
芸術研究にかかわる活動の助成及び振興 [Support and promotion of art research activities]
CD, I: ひびのこづえ Kodue Hibino　AD: ナガクラトモヒコ Tomohiko Nagakura
D: 宮崎 史 Fumi Miyazaki　Planner: 森 司 Tsukasa Mori　PR: 守屋その子 Sonoko Moriya
SB: サン・アド Sun-Ad

others 175

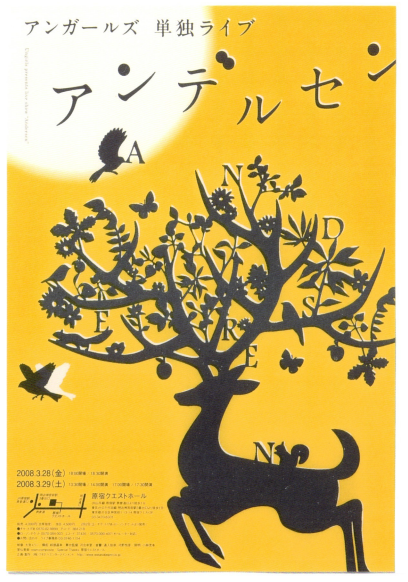

ワタナベエンターテインメント
WATANABE ENTERTAINMENT
芸能事務所 [Talent agency]
AD, D: カイシトモヤ Tomoya Kaishi　I: 酒井博子 Hiroko Sakai
DF, SB: ルームコンポジット room-composite

チラシ Flyer

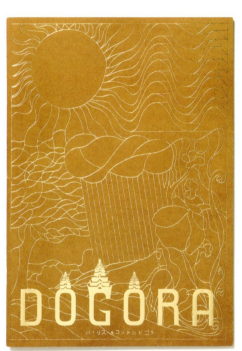
パンフレット Pamphlet

アルバトロス・フィルム ALBATROS FILM
映画配給 [Film distributor]
AD, D, Artwork: 柿木原政広 Masahiro Kakinokihara
Artwork: 大塚いちお Ichio Orsuka
Producer: 横山浩子 Hiroko Yokoyama SB: 10

HOP ハウジングオペレーション HOP Housing Operation
工務店、建築士事務所 [Contractor / architect's office]
AD, D: 寺島賢幸 Masayuki Terashima
DF, SB: 寺島デザイン制作室 TERASHIMA DESIGN

秋ざんまい、しましょう。
ENJOY! Marunouchi Autumn 2008

others 179

丸の内に、セールという花が咲きました。
Marunouchi SUMMER SALE
2008 7.1 TUE – 7.13 SUN

この夏が、
あの夏になりますように。
Summer 2008

丸ビル・新丸ビル Marunouchi Building / Shin-marunouchi Building
複合商業施設 [Shopping complex]
AD: 廣村正彰 Masaaki Hiromura　D: 中尾千絵 Chie Nakao / 黄 善佳 Songa Fan
P: KAZ ARAHAMA　CW: 松木圭三 Keizo Matsuki
Stylist: 飯島朋子 Tomoko Iijima　DF: 廣村デザイン事務所 Hiromura Design Office
SB: 丸ビル・新丸ビル Marunouchi Building / Shin-marunouchi Building

高知県立牧野植物園 The Kochi Prefectural Makino Botanical Garden
植物園 [Botanical Garden]
D. I: 岡林里佳　Rika Okabayashi
SB: 高知県立牧野植物園　The Kochi Prefectural Makino Botanical Garden

others

電飾看板 Sign of illumination

恵比寿ガーデンプレイス YEBISU GARDEN PLACE
商業施設 [Shopping complex]
AD, D: カイシトモヤ Tomoya Kaishi　I: Murgraph
CW: 東海林美佳 Mika Tokairin　DF, SB: ルームコンポジット room-composite

DESIGN FOR MANKIND
アート・デザインのウェブサイト [Art / Design Website]
CD, AD, CW: Erin Loechner　D: Ken Loechner　DF, SB: DESIGN FOR MANKIND

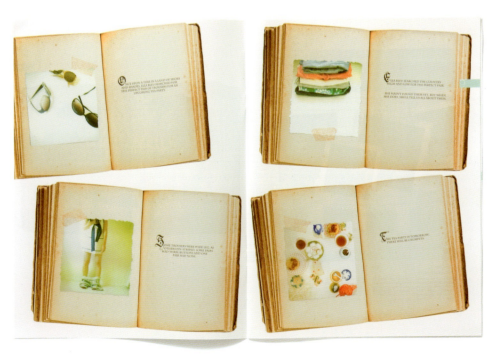

雑誌 Magazine

ポスター Posters

J-WAVE
ラジオ局 [Radio station]
CD: 嶋 浩一郎 Koichiro Shima　AD: 寄藤文平 Bunpei Yorifuji
D: 坂野達也 Tatsuya Sakano
PL: 石原 篤 Atsushi Ishihara ／ 加藤晋吾 Shingo Kato ／ 峰 典子 Noriko Mine
PR: 神谷淳一 Junichi Kamiya　DF, SB: 博報堂ケトル Hakuhodo Kettle

販促ツール Promotion tool

others 183

ダイレクトメール DM

ぴあ / ユーロスペース Pia Corporation / Eurospace
映画配給　[Film distributor]
AD, SB: 大島依提亜　Idea Oshima

パンフレット　Pamphlet

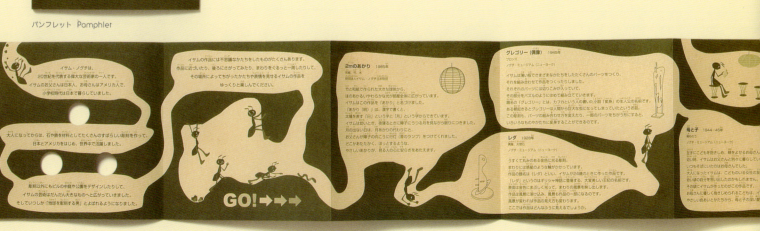

東京都現代美術館　MOT
美術館　[Museum]
AD, I: 山下浩平　Kohei Yamashita　SB: マウンテンマウンテン　mountain mountain

宝塚造形芸術大学 Takarazuka University
大学 [University]
AD: 藤脇慎吾 Shingo Fujiwaki D, SB: 渡部みなみ Minami Watanabe

東武百貨店 TOBU DEPARTMENT STORE
百貨店事業 [Department store]
AD: 今井クミ Kumi Imai D: 金子朋世 Tomoyo Kaneko CW: 遠藤真由美 Mayumi Endo
DF, SB: アピスラボラトリー APIS LABORATORY

ラフラ rafra
アクセサリー作家 [Accessary designer]
AD, D: 相澤徳行 Noriyuki Aizawa DF, SB: 相澤デザイン室 Aizawa Design

SPRING

AUTUMN

SUMMER

WINTER

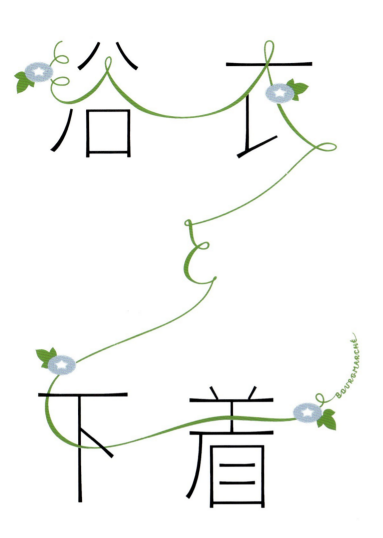

ワコール Wacoal Corporation
アンダーウェアブランド [Lingerie Brand]
CD: 宮田 諭 Satoru Miyata　AD, D: 関本明子 Akiko Sekimoto
CW: 岡山真子 Shinko Okayama　PR: 中岡美奈子 Minako Nakaoka
DF, SB: ドラフト　DRAFT

→ P.032
和み Nagomi
お茶の製造・販売 [Tea maker]
CD, AD, D: 関 宙明 Hiroaki Seki　DF, SB: ミスター・ユニバース mr.universe

ぴあ / ユーロスペース Pia Corporation / Eurospace
映画配給・宣伝 [Film distributor]
AD, SB: 大島依提亜 Idea Oshima

ハウステンボス HUIS TEN BOSCH
ホテル経営 [Hotel management]
CD, AD: 今井クミ Kumi Imai　D: 橋詰千春 Chiharu Hashizume
CW: 後藤国弘 Kunihiro Goto　DF, SB: アピスラボラトリー APIS LABORATORY

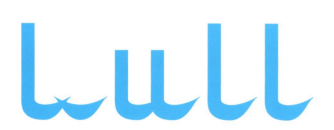

Lull
ヨットクラブ [Yacht club]
AD, D, SB: 篠塚太郎 Taro Shinozuka

→ P.152
Green Genes
子ども服・小物ブティック
[Eco-friendly boutique specializing in green goodies for children]
D: Eric Kass   DF, SB: Funnel: Eric Kass: Utilitarian + Commercial + Fine Art

→ P.108
グリュック glück
美容室 [Beauty salon]
CD, AD: 新ヶ江友也 Tomoya Shingae   AD, D: 熊谷由紀 Yuki Kumagae

ジオサーフ Geosurf
モバイルマッピング・ソリューションの開発・販売・コンサルティング
[Mobile mapping solutions development, sales, and consulting]
AD, D, DF, SB: アトリエタイク ateliertaik

Coordinators 2
養子縁組斡旋 [Adoption Agency]
D, I, SB: Lizette Gecel   I: Eric Knight

Virginia League of Planned Parenthood
医療施設 [Women's Reproductive Healthcare Center]
D, I, SB: Lizette Gecel

→ P.118
小原流 OHARA SCHOOL of IKEBANA
生け花の学校 [School of Ikebana]
AD: 永田武史 Takeshi Nagata   D: 鹿島絵美 Emi Kashima / 田代奈々 Nana Tashiro
SB: エヌ・デザイン enudesign

→ P.058
ルーペ Loupe
洋菓子製造・販売 [Confectionary manufacture and sales]
AD, D: 成澤 豪 Go Narisawa   D, I: 成澤宏美 Hiromi Narisawa
DF, SB: なかよし図工室 Nakayoshi Zukoushitsu

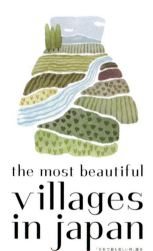

NPO「日本で最も美しい村」連合
The most beautiful villages in Japan
NPO 団体 [NPO]
SB: NPO「日本で最も美しい村」連合
The most beautiful villages in Japan

George Fox University
大学 [College]
CD, AD, D, I: Jeff Fisher
DF, SB: Jeff Fisher Logo Motives

Bella Terra Landscape Design
景観デザイナー [Landscape Designer]
CD, AD, D, I: Jeff Fisher
DF, SB: Jeff Fisher Logo Motives

提供社リスト / Submitter list

国内 / Japan

あ

相澤デザイン室　Aizawa Design 22, 186
アサツーディ・ケイ　ASATSU-DK 34, 168
アトリエタイク　atelierraik 64, 65, 171, 188
アピスラボラトリー　APIS LABORATORY 56, 102, 170, 186, 187
アリエルトレーディング　Ariel Trading 80
アルビオン　ALBION 88, 96
E 114
イッカクイッカ　Ikkakuikka 106
イデアインターナショナル　IDEA International 72
インナチュラル　IN NATURAL 90
インフォバーン　INFOBAHN 138
上平稔人デザイン室　Minoru Uehira Design Office 113, 148
エージー　AZ 27
エヌ・ジー　N.G 160
エヌ・デザイン　enudesign 118, 127, 189
NPO「日本で最も美しい村」連合
The most beautiful villages in Japan 189
大島依提亜　Oshima Idea 101, 183, 139, 187

か

花王　Kao Corporation 94
カナリア　Canaria 12
カルビー　Calbee Foods 24
キンザ座　Kinzaza 115
薬日本堂　NIHONDO 84
高知県立牧野植物園
The Kochi Prefectural Makino Botanical Garden 180
コミューン　COMMUNE 126

さ

SAGA 16
佐藤晃一　Sato Koichi 140
ザ・ボディショップ　THE BODY SHOP 78
サン・アド　Sun-Ad 35, 38, 40, 99, 174
サンエー・インターナショナル　SANEI-INTERNATIONAL 98

篠塚大郎　Shinozuka Taro 188
JS.WORKS 104
清水正己デザイン事務所　shimizu masami design office 134
ジュリーク・ジャパン　Jurlique Japan 82
昭文社　Shobunsha Publications 141
スーパーミー　Super me 107
スターバックス コーヒー ジャパン　Starbucks Coffee Japan 61
ストライド　STRIDE 143, 160, 172

た

ダイキン工業　DAIKIN INDUSTORIES 132
大黒大悟　Daikoku Daigo 108, 109, 112, 113
TUGBOAT2 136
玉の肌石鹸　TAMANOHADA 95
タルゴジャボン　Thalgo Japon 48
月岡正明　Tsukioka Masaaki 91
Tea note 44
デポ　Des Pors 153
寺島デザイン制作室　TERASHIMA DESIGN 49, 114, 176
10 177
ドラフト　DRAFT 121, 125, 187

な

中塚広告事務所　Nakatsuka & Partners 68
なかよし図工室　Nakayoshi Zukoushitsu 50, 58, 63, 65, 162, 189
日産自動車　NISSAN MOTOR 120
日本ベリエールアートセンター　Japan Belier Art Center 36
ネオス　NEOS 41

は

博報堂ケトル　Hakuhodo Kettle 182
林タオル フランジュール事業部
HAYASHI TOWEL FRANCJOUR DIV 86
PANGAEA 100, 163
ビーエルティー　BLT 46

P913 42
ピーコン・コミュニケーションズ heacon communications 25
ピリカインターナショナル Pilica International Japan 74
ビルド・クリエイティブハウス BUILD creativehaus 122, 167
フィッツコーポレーション FITS Corporation 76
福島デザイン FUKUSHIMA DESIGN 26
プラザスタイル PLAZASTYLE 70
フレッシュアンドフレッシュジャパン Fresh & Fresh Japan 60

ま
マウンテンマウンテン mountain mountain 183
マッキャンエリクソン MacCann Erickson Japan 23
マヒコ Mahiko 156
丸ビル・新丸ビル
Marunouchi Building / Shin-marunouchi Building 178
三木 健デザイン事務所 Ken Miki & Associates 166, 173
MR_DESIGN 14
ミスター・ユニバース mr.universe 32, 129, 142, 150, 187
ミナ ペルホネン minä perhonen 103
メディア・エーシー Media AC 171
メルクロス MERCROS 128
MOTTAINAIキャンペーン MOTTAINAI Campaign 130

や
ヨーガンレール Jurgen Lehl 105

ら
ルームコンポジット room-composite 175, 181

わ
渡部みなみ Watanabe Minami 186

海外 / Overseas

B
BB/Saunders 164
Brandient 147, 167
BVD 30, 75, 151

D
DELPHINE 152
DESIGN FOR MANKIND 181

F
Firefly Tonics 28
Funnel: Eric Kass: Utilitarian + Commercial + Fine: Art
....28, 151, 188

G
Gruppe Gut 165

H
Hornall Anderson 29, 79
Hyperakt 144, 146, 147

J
Jeff Fisher Logo Motives 189

L
Lizette Gecel 139, 189

M
MacCann Erickson, Mumbai 62
MOZI 47

P
Pati Núñez Associats 31, 54, 92
Paul Cartwright Branding 95

S
SPATCHURST 165

T
The Sorrell Company 139
Turner Duckworth: London & San Francisco
..............................18, 20, 45, 51, 52, 93, 124

ナチュラルスタイル グラフィックス
Relaxing Graphics　Warm, Calm, Exhilarating

JACKET & COVER DESIGN

ART DIRECTOR: 永田武史（エヌ・デザイン）　Takeshi Nagata (enudesign)
DESIGNER: 倉田ゆりえ（エヌ・デザイン）　Yurie Kurata (enudesign)
PHOTOGRAPHER: 中島宏樹　Hiroki Nakashima
STYLIST: 青木もえ　Moe Aoki
RETOUCHER: 千原光一　Koichi Chihara

ART DIRECTOR: 柴 亜季子　Akiko Shiba
DESIGNER: 高松 セリア サユリ　Célia Sayuri Takamatsu
PHOTOGRAPHER: 藤本邦治　Kuniharu Fujimoto
TRANSLATOR: パメラ ミキ　Pamela Miki
EDITOR: 瀧 亮子　Akiko Taki
COORDINATOR: 岸田麻矢　Maya A. Kishida
PLANNER: 高橋かおる　Kaoru Takahashi
PUBLISHER: 三芳伸吾　Shingo Miyoshi

2008年12月16日　初版第1刷発行

発行所　ピエ・ブックス
〒170-0005　東京都豊島区南大塚 2-32-4
編集　Tel: 03-5395-4820　Fax: 03-5395-4821
e-mail: editor@piebooks.com
営業　Tel: 03-5395-4811　Fax: 03-5395-4812
e-mail: sales@piebooks.com
http://www.piebooks.com

印刷・製本　（株）サンニチ印刷

©2008 PIE BOOKS
ISBN978-4-89444-736-3 C3070
Printed in Japan

本書の収録内容の無断転載、複写、引用を禁じます。
落丁、乱丁はお取り替え致します。